SCHIRMER PERFORMANCE EDITIONS

THE 20TH CENTURY
Early Intermediate Level

27 Pieces by Bartók, Kabalevsky,
Khachaturian, Shostakovich and Others
in Progressive Order

Compiled and Edited by Richard Walters

On the cover:
People at Night, Guided by the Phosphorescent Tracks of Snails (1940)
by Joan Miró (1893–1983)
Philadelphia Museum of Art, Pennsylvania, PA, USA
The Louis E. Stern Collection, 1963 / Bridgeman Images
© Successió Miró / Artists Rights Society (ARS), New York / ADAGP, Paris 2015

ISBN 978-1-4950-1023-1

G. SCHIRMER, Inc.

DISTRIBUTED BY
HAL•LEONARD®
CORPORATION
7777 W. BLUEMOUND RD. P.O. BOX 13819 MILWAUKEE, WI 53213

www.musicsalesclassical.com
www.halleonard.com

CONTENTS

Though the table of contents appears in alphabetical order by composer, the music in this book is in progressive order.

COMPOSER BIOGRAPHIES, HISTORICAL NOTES
AND
PRACTICE AND PERFORMANCE TIPS

The pieces in this collection are by some of the greatest composers of the 20th century, composers who wrote a full range of music for orchestra, voices, piano, and chamber ensembles, in the great and large forms. But they also valued music education, and composed interesting music to foster a student pianist's progress. The music by these composers leads a student not only to technical proficiency, but also to become a more fully formed, imaginative musician. Some of these pieces challenge a student to broaden experience beyond conventional, traditional harmony and rhythm. In these works a piano student gets a glimpse into the mind of a great, forward-thinking artistic genius.

In the 20th century composers generally conceived every detail in a composition (unless it is left to chance by design). Many students do not seem to understand the organic role that slurs, phrases, staccatos, accents, dynamics, pedaling, and changes of tempo play in a 20th century composition. Tempo, articulation and dynamics are in mind from the outset of composition, as essential to the music as are the notes and rhythms.

In earlier centuries it was not the custom for the composer to necessarily notate all articulation and pedaling. Insightful understanding of period style of playing informs many of these details in music from the Baroque and Classical eras. Even in music of the 19th century composers did not always notate all such details, and a player's understanding of style is necessary in adding things implied but not stated in the score. Most composers of the 20th century became much more specific about notating such matters. Almost without exception, articulations and dynamics are not editorial suggestions in *The 20th Century* series. They are by the composer and part of the composition. If editorial suggestions are very occasionally made, they are specifically noted on a piece or indicated in brackets.

Pedaling in *The 20th Century* series is by the composer unless indicated otherwise on an individual piece. Fingering is also often by the composer. Metronome indications without brackets are by the composer. In works where the composer did not provide a suggested metronome indication, those in brackets are editorial suggestions.

The "Practice and Performance Tips" point out a few ideas that may be helpful to the student in learning a piece. These might also be used by a busy teacher as an at-a-glance look at some topics in teaching a piece.

The pieces as part of sets for "children" are actually for progressing pianists of any age. Composers needed a way to indicate to the world that the pieces were written for a contained level of difficulty and for students, and were to be thought of differently from concert works such as a sonata or concerto, for example. The tradition of titling these with some variation along the lines of a "children's album" was a convenient way of solving this. It has always been understood, and certainly by the composers themselves, that this music is about the level of the pianist, not the age of the pianist.

When a great talent turns attention to writing a short piece of limited difficulty level for students, it is approached with the same aesthetics, temperament, tastes and creative invention applied when composing a symphony, opera or concerto. These exquisite miniatures are complete works of timeless art. Through them a master musician of the past indirectly teaches a progressing musician of the present and the future.

GEORGE ANTHEIL
(1900–1959, American)

After studying with Constantin von Sternberg in Philadelphia and Ernest Bloch in New York, American composer George Antheil moved to Berlin in 1922. He travelled around Europe as a concert pianist, often performing his own works. In 1923 he moved to Paris, where he became a prominent member of the avant-garde, befriending James Joyce, Ezra Pound, W.B. Yeats, Erik Satie and Pablo Picasso. His most famous piece is *Ballet méchanique* (1925), scored for multiple pianos, player pianos, percussion, siren, and two propellers. Due to the difficulty of executing a piece of such magnitude, it is known more theoretically than for actual performance. Antheil's earlier works, such as the *Ballet méchanique*, were often jazz-inspired, experimental and jarringly mechanistic. In the 1940s, back in the United States, Antheil turned to a more conventional style. A virtuoso concert pianist, he composed more for piano than any other instrument.

Sad from *La femme 100 têtes* (composed 1933)
La femme 100 têtes (literally translated The Woman 100 Heads) is a set of 45 preludes inspired by surrealist etchings of Max Ernst, published in a book titled *La femme 100 têtes*.

Practice and Performance Tips
- Choose a tempo that is in the spirit of the title, "Sad." Do not play this piece too quickly.
- Even though it is slow and expressive, keep a steady beat throughout.
- Shape a graceful, long phrase: measures. 2–5, 6–7, 10–13, 14–17, 18–19.
- The composer's dynamic markings, indicating crescendos and decrescendos, show how he intends the music to be phrased.
- The pedaling in this edition is an editorial suggestion. This piece needs pedaling, but there are other solutions. Whatever pedaling you use, the aim is to clarify rhythm and harmony. Do not let the music sound blurred.
- Stress the expressive dissonances in measures 11–12.

BÉLA BARTÓK
(1881–1945, Hungarian; became a US citizen in 1945)

Béla Bartók is one of the most important and often performed composers of the twentieth century, and much of his music, including *Concerto for Orchestra*, his concertos, his string quartets, and his opera *Bluebeard's Castle*, holds a venerable position in the classical repertoire. His parents were amateur musicians who nurtured their young son with exposure to dance music, drumming, and piano lessons. In 1899 he started piano and composition studies at the Academy of Music in Budapest and not long after graduation he joined the Academy's piano faculty. Bartók wished to create music that was truly Hungarian at its core, a desire that sparked his deep interest in folk music. His work collecting and studying folksongs from around the Baltic region impacted his own compositional style greatly in terms of rhythm, mood, and texture. Bartók utilized folk influences to create a truly unique style. Though he composed opera, concertos, ballets, and chamber music, he was also committed to music education and composed several piano works for students, including his method *Mikrokosmos*. Bartók toured extensively in the 1920s and '30s, and became as well-known as both a pianist and composer. He immigrated to the US in 1940 to escape war and political turmoil in Europe, and settled in New York City, though the last years of his life were difficult, with many health problems.

Selections from *Ten Easy Pieces*, Sz. 39, BB 51
(composed 1908)
Bartók collected and documented thousands of folksongs from Hungary and neighboring countries. This folk music influenced his own compositions throughout his subsequent career, but especially in the initial years of its impact, 1904–1910. Bartók made "art music" settings of folksongs, and also created compositions that are in the spirit of folk music. It is often not clear which of these is at work in a piece by Bartók, because the composer didn't necessarily document which pieces were based on folksongs and which are original compositions in that style. This approach applies to *Ten Easy Pieces*.

Painful Scuffle
Practice and Performance Tips
- Be careful not to take this brooding music too quickly.
- Practice left hand alone, creating a smooth, even line.
- It may help some students to begin by practicing the left hand *mf*, then move to *p* and *pp* when comfortable with the pattern.
- Bartók asks for *molto espressivo* in the right hand melody. Note the "hairpin" rise and fall in dynamics.
- Practice the right-hand melody alone, observing all the details of dynamics and phrase to make it expressive.
- Divide the piece into sections for practice. For instance, section 1: measures 1–10; section 2: measures 11–22.
- The smoothness of this music needs to be accomplished with the fingers. Use no sustaining pedal.
- It is very important that the tempo remains very steady, until it slows down in the final measures.
- The term *calando* means decreasing in volume and speed.

Slovak Peasant Dance
Practice and Performance Tips
- Guard against playing this piece too aggressively. Note that it is primarily quiet playing.
- Quiet, crisp staccato playing predominates.

- It may help some students to learn this music at a *mf* before mastering a soft touch in sections marked *p* and *pp*.
- Begin with slow practice, either hands separately or together.
- Learn the articulation from the beginning, as you learn the notes and rhythms.
- Divide the piece into sections for practice. For instance, section 1: measures 1–10; section 2: measures 11–21; section 3: measures 22–30; section 4: measures 31–44; section 5: measures 45–54.
- As you master the music, increase your practice speed, but always maintaining steadiness at any tempo.
- At *poco sostenuto* (a little more sustained) in measure 42 you can play a very slight *ritard*.
- Keep a smooth left hand in measures 47–52, with staccato in the right hand.
- Use no pedal at all.

Selections from *For Children*, Sz. 42, BB 53
(composed 1908–09)

Bartók was one of the pioneering ethnomusicologists in eastern Europe, collecting and documenting thousands of folksongs from Hungary and neighboring countries. The original edition of *For Children* was in four volumes. Volumes 1–2 were compositions based on Hungarian folk songs. Volumes 3–4 were compositions based on Slovakian folk songs. Bartók created a revised edition in 1943, with only minor changes to the original regarding compositional content, with the pieces retitled. Some pieces were eliminated for the revised edition, and the four volumes were consolidated into two. In the preface to *For Children* Bartók wrote that the pieces were designed to teach young players "the simple and non-Romantic beauties of folk music."

Children's Dance (Volume 1)

From Volume 1 in the original four volume edition, with the English title "Round Dance." Bartók changed the title for the revised edition.

Practice and Performance Tips
- Begin by practicing hands alone and without pedal, starting at a slow tempo.
- Pay careful attention to the accents when practicing the left hand alone.
- When practicing the right hand alone pay careful attention to the slurs and accents.
- For this piece in particular, we recommend left hand alone as you increase the practice tempo.
- Only when each hand is mastered should you move into practicing hands together, first at a slow tempo.
- Divide the piece into sections for practice. Section 1: measures 1–20; section 2: measures 21–48.
- The slanted lines at the end of measure 20 indicate a *cesura* (sometimes also spelled caesura), a short break before continuing on.

- Do not slow down before the *cesura*.
- Do not attempt the composer's pedaling until you are practicing the piece at a near performance tempo.
- Bartók's pedaling is very specific. Take note!
- Do not speed up as you play, no matter what the tempo.
- Even though the music is fast and loud, note that it is also legato.

Children's Game (Volume 1)

From Volume 1 in the original four volume edition, with the English title "Alone in the Rain." Bartók changed the title for the revised edition.

Practice and Performance Tips
- Bartók's setting of a Hungarian folksong for children is full of vivid details.
- Practice slowly, hands separately.
- Be careful to learn exactly the staccatos, slurs and accents throughout, with special attention to the right hand melody.
- The quarter-note chords and notes marked with staccato/tenuto should be played roughly as eighth notes followed by eighth rests, not with the shortness of regular staccato.
- When moving to slow practice with hands together, retain all the articulation detail learned when practicing hands alone.
- The piece has three verses. The right-hand melody is different each time. Pay attention!
- Practice each verse separately as a section, taking care to notice the differences in each verse.
- Notice how the left-hand "accompaniment" varies in each verse.
- The verses are separated by the simple, quiet Adagio section.
- Do not rush through the full measures of rest (measures 21, 26, 47, 52).
- Use no pedal at all.

Study for the Left Hand (Volume 1)

From Volume 1 of the original four volume edition, with the English title "The Flowers Sing of Love." Bartók changed the title for the revised edition.

Practice and Performance Tips
- Even though the melody is in the right hand, even by the title of the piece Bartók calls attention to the left hand.
- The challenge is to keep the wrist loose and without tension while playing the repeated notes in the left hand.
- If your left hand becomes tense while practicing, you need to stop, rotate your wrist, and loosen up before playing again.
- You might try practicing the left hand at a slower tempo, and gradually increase speed while keeping the wrist loose.

- Bartók's original fingering, used here, introduces the student to repeated notes in the right hand played by different fingers.
- It is very important to keep a steady beat throughout. Avoid speeding up!
- To keep the musical texture interesting, Bartók has added accents in the left hand on the downbeats of measures 20, 22 and 24.
- When practicing the right hand alone pay careful attention to the articulation Bartók has composed.
- Note that Bartók has marked the right hand *molto marcato* (heavily accented short staccato), but the left hand is marked only staccato.
- The slanted lines at the end of measure 40 indicate a *cesura* (sometimes also spelled *caesura*), a short break before continuing on.
- Do not slow down before the *cesura*.
- Pay close attention to the dynamic changes Bartók has composed.
- Do not slow down at the end. Stay in tempo and fade away to as softly as you can play.
- Use no pedal in this piece. Pedaling would be completely wrong for its texture.

Forest Nymph (Volume 2)

From Volume 3 in the original four volume edition. The title in English, "Forest Nymph" comes from the original edition. The piece is untitled (No. 23) in the revised edition.

Practice and Performance Tips
- Become acquainted with the Slovakian folk melody by practicing right hand alone.
- Pay close attention to the phrasing and articulation Bartók has composed for the right-hand melody.
- Be sure to play the sixteenth note followed by the dotted eighth note (as on the downbeats of measures 1–4) gently and not too aggressively. Note the *p* dynamic.
- Think of the quarter-note chords in the left hand with a staccato/tenuto as being played as an eighth note followed by an eighth rest.
- The *sostenuto* marking in measure 8 indicates that the music slows a bit until the *a tempo* in measure 12.
- Keep the left hand smooth and quiet in measures 13–16.
- Bartók's *sonore* indication in measure 19 means to play more sustained and with a fuller tone, but not *f*.
- Only use the sustaining pedal in the spot Bartók has indicated, measure 10.

PAUL CRESTON
(1906–1985, American)

Paul Creston was born into a poor Italian immigrant family in New York. As a child he took piano and organ lessons but was self-taught in theory and composition.

In 1938 Creston was awarded a Guggenheim Fellowship, and in 1941 the New York Music Critics' Circle Award. He served as the director of A.S.C.A.P. from 1960–1968, and was composer-in-residence and professor of music at Central Washington State College from 1968–1975. His works, which include additions to orchestral, vocal, piano, and chamber music repertoire, often feature shifting rhythmic patterns. He wrote a number of solos for instruments customarily left out of the limelight, such as the marimba, accordion, or saxophone. Creston was an important composition teacher (John Corigliano studied with him), and also wrote the books *Principles of Rhythm* and *Rational Metric Notation*.

Toy Dance from *Five Little Dances*, Op. 24, No. 3
(composed 1940)
Practice and Performance Tips
- Most important is the composer's indication of "very crisp."
- Except for some occasional slurred notes in the right hand, the entire piece is played staccato.
- Begin practice hands alone, playing at a slow tempo.
- Learn the articulation from the beginning, along with the notes and rhythms.
- Divide the piece into sections for practice. For instance, section 1: measures 1–10; section 2: measures 11–20; section 3: measures 21–28; section 4: measures 29–36.
- This music needs to be played very evenly and steadily.
- Do not take the tempo too quickly. Find quarter note = 126 on a metronome.
- "Stiffly" does not mean that your hand should be stiff in playing!
- Except for the outburst of *f* in measures 31–32, and the final phrase in measures 35–36, this music is to be played softly.
- It may help in early stages of practice to play the *p* sections at *mf*, then move to *p* when you have mastered the music.
- Use no pedal at all. Pedaling would spoil the crispness required.

MORTON GOULD
(1913–1996, American)

Morton Gould was born in Queens to an Australian father and a Russian mother. He composed his first work, a waltz for piano, when he was six. At eight he entered the Institute of Musical Art, which would later become the Juilliard School. His first work was published by G. Schirmer in 1932 when he was eighteen. Gould was a distinctly American presence, writing in both popular and contemporary classical styles and proving himself adept at conquering the rising mediums of radio and cinema. In the 1930s he played piano in vaudeville acts and at cinemas and dance studies. For radio he composed commercial jingles and radio symphonettes, and he also worked as a conductor, arranger, and composer for WOR New York's weekly "Music for Today" program. In 1933, Stokowski premiered his Chorale and Fugue in Jazz with the Philadelphia Orchestra. Gould wrote in various styles and blurred the lines between classical and popular music. Besides concert works he also wrote for Broadway. His works were performed by the New York Philharmonic, the Cleveland Orchestra other leading orchestras. In 1994 he was awarded a Kennedy Center Honor for his contributions to American culture, and in 1995 he won the Pulitzer Prize for his final orchestral work, Stringmusic, which he wrote on commission for the National Symphony Orchestra as a farewell to Mstislav Rostropovich.

Birthday Bells from *At the Piano,* Book 1
(composed 1964)

At the Piano (Books 1 and 2) was written for Gould's daughter Deborah as she studied piano.

Practice and Performance Tips
- Begin practice hands together at a slow tempo.
- As you master the music, increase the tempo in your practice, but always keep it steady, whatever the tempo.
- Your final performance tempo should be determined by how fast you can gracefully manage the parallel fourths in the left hand in measures 29–30.
- The composer's words "loud and happy" apply to the sections marked *f* and *ff* only.
- The composer has written, "Use plenty of pedal!" We have made an editorial suggestion of pedaling beyond this.

ALAN HOVHANNESS
(1911–2000, American)

Alan Hovhaness was born in Somerville, Massachusetts, and studied at the New England Conservatory with Frederick Converse. He became interested in the music of India, to which he was exposed by musicians in the Boston area, and later looked to his Armenian heritage as well as music from Japan and Korea for inspiration. A prolific composer, Hovhaness' over five hundred works include all the major genres of western art music. He wrote six ballets as well as other stage works, sixty-six symphonies, works for chorus and voice, and numerous chamber and piano pieces. One of his most well-known works is his Symphony No. 2 *Mysterious Mountain*, premiered by Leopold Stokowski and the Philadelphia Orchestra in 1955. His career went through a number of stages, incorporating aspects from the Renaissance and the Romantic era in addition to traditions outside Western classical music.

Despite these shifts in style, he consistently sought to portray a connection between music, spirituality, and nature. Mountains particularly moved him, and he chose to live much of his life in Switzerland and the Pacific Northwest due to the proximity of these regions to the landscape that served as his muse.

Moon Dance from *Mountain Idylls,* Op. 119, No. 2
(composed 1931, 1949, 1955)

This set was subtitled "Three Easy Pieces for Piano." Published as set in 1955, the three pieces were written at various times. An idyll is a poem describing a pastoral, simple scene. Hovhaness was particularly fond of mountains. "Moon Dance" is the easiest of the three pieces in the set.

Practice and Performance Tips
- Practice slowly hands separately.
- Practice the right-hand melody, finding the phrasing and singing tone.
- Practice the left hand, creating the quiet and smooth movement of the broken triads.
- The piece asks for soft but sparkling tone. Imagine the gentle glistening of moonlight.
- Practice the pedaling Hovhaness has composed while practicing the left hand alone.
- As you master the piece, move on to the *Allegro* tempo. Keep a steady beat throughout.

DMITRI KABALEVSKY
(1904–1987, Russian)

Kabalevsky was an important Russian composer of the Soviet era who wrote music in many genres, including four symphonies, a handful of operas, theatre and film scores, patriotic music, choral music, vocal music, and numerous piano works. He embraced the Soviet notion of socialist realism in art, a fact that was more than politically advantageous to his career in the USSR. While studying piano and composition at the Moscow Conservatory, he taught piano lessons at a music college and it was for these students that he began writing works for young players. In 1932 he began teaching at the Moscow Conservatory, earning the title of professor in 1939. He eventually went on to develop programs for the concert hall, radio, and television aimed at teaching children about classical music. In the last decades of his life, Kabalevsky focused on developing music curricula for schools, retiring from the Moscow Conservatory to teach in public schools where he could test his theories and the effectiveness of his syllabi. This he considered his true life's work, and his pedagogical principles revolutionized music education in Russia. A collection of his writings on music education was published in English in 1988 as *Music and Education: A Composer Writes About Musical Education.*

Selections from *30 Pieces for Children*, Op. 27 (composed 1937–38)

Kabalevsky often quoted Maxim Gorki, saying that books for children should be "the same as for adults, only better." Kabalevsky believed strongly in writing music for young players that was not dumbed-down, but rather, complete, imaginative compositions unto themselves. Kabalevsky did a slight revision of Op. 27 in 1985, which was intended to be an authoritative edition. (This is our source for the pieces in this collection.)

Playing Ball, Op. 27, No. 5
Practice and Performance Tips
- This music requires a playful, light touch.
- Kabalevsky has composed a study in changing hand positions, moving down or up the keyboard.
- The moving hand positions, as well as the changes from major to minor, represent tossing a ball back and forth.
- Begin practice hands together and slowly.
- Anticipate where your hands will move in the next measure.
- Increase your practice tempo only when you have mastered the music.
- Carefully observe the dynamic shifts.
- Divide the piece into sections for practice. For instance, section 1: measures 1–16; section 2: measures 17–24; section 3, measures 25–38; section 4: measures 39–54.
- Kabalevsky has indicated pedaling only and specifically for the quarter-note/eighth-note combination in measures 8, 18, 20, 22, etc. Otherwise, use no pedal.
- A performance should have a crisp, fun spirit about it.

Toccatina, Op. 27, No. 12
Practice and Performance Tips
- A *toccata* is a piece that shows brilliant playing. A *toccatina* is a miniature *toccata*.
- The left-hand melody should be predominant, marked *cantando* (singing), and played smoothly.
- The right-hand staccato chords are accompaniment to the left-hand melody.
- Practice the right hand separately, playing the chords crisply.
- Begin practice slowly, learning the phrasing, articulation and dynamics as you learn the notes and rhythms.
- Divide the piece into sections for practice. For instance, section 1: measures 1–18; section 2: measures 19–34; section 3: measures 35–49.
- Only increase the speed when you have mastered all the details.
- Do not play this music (marked *allegretto*) too quickly.
- Use no pedal throughout. Pedaling would blur the staccato chords in the right hand.

Sonatina, Op. 27, No. 18
Practice and Performance Tips
- Except for measure 41, the left hand is an accompaniment throughout to the right-hand melody.
- Begin practice hands separately at a slow tempo.
- Learn the phrasing as composed as you learn the right-hand melody.
- Even though the opening motive is rhythmic and rigorous, note that Kabalevsky has written a phrase over it.
- The staccato chords in the left hand should be played crisply.
- Divide the piece into sections for practice. For instance, section 1: measures 1–12; section 2: measures 13–24; section 3: measures 25–32; section 4: measures 33–43.
- Note the sudden shifts to *p* in measures 13 and 33.
- The only spots requiring pedal are as marked, measure 7 and measure 31, with the rolled chord in the left hand.
- Other than as marked, use no pedal.

A Short Story from *24 Pieces for Children*, Op. 39, No. 22
Practice and Performance Tips
- Kabalevsky is teaching independence of the hands in this composition.
- The left-hand melody is smooth, with longer phrases throughout.
- The right-hand accompaniment is staccato throughout.
- The left-hand melody should be prominent; the right-hand accompaniment should be less conspicuous.
- Begin practice slowly for this *allegro assai* (quite fast) piece.
- Divide the piece into sections for practice. For instance, section 1: measures 1–19; section 2: measures 20–37; section 3: measures 37–49.
- Learn the articulation, different in each hand, from the beginning of practice.
- Increase the speed only when you have mastered notes, articulations, dynamics and all details.
- Use no pedal at all.

Selections from *35 Easy Pieces*, Op. 89 (composed 1972–74)

Kabalevsky's last large set of piano pieces for students was composed in his late sixties, after a lifetime of experiences with young musicians, and after he had attained a revered position as the cultural leader of music education in the USSR. These were also his last works for piano. After 1974 Kabalevsky only wrote a few more compositions, which were songs or small choral pieces.

Rabbit Teasing a Bear-Cub, Op. 89, No. 31
Practice and Performance Tips
- The right hand represents the quick movements of the rabbit.

- The left hand represents the slower, less coordinated movements of the bear cub.
- First practice hands alone separately, learning all the details of articulation.
- When putting hands together in practice, retain all the details of articulation mastered in hands alone practice.
- Pay careful attention to the dynamics, which help create the character and scene.
- Measure 9 is where the rabbit is most annoying to the bear.
- In the last line of the music it's as if the rabbit has gone too far in annoying the bear and is scampering away.
- Performing a character piece such as this needs wit and fun. Let the imagery of the rabbit and bear help you create a colorful performance.
- Use no pedal at all.

Almost a Waltz, Op. 89, No. 33
Practice and Performance Tips

- In the meter changes the composer has indicated how the measure divides.
- 7/4 measures (most of the piece) are a combination of 4 beats + 3 beats, indicated by the dotted bar line.
- 6/4 measures are a combination of 3 beats + 3 beats, indicated by the dotted bar line.
- Because the quarter note stays the same throughout, these meters are not difficult to comprehend.
- Keep the quarter-note beat steady throughout, except in the section marked *poco rit.*
- *Cantando* means singing, applied to the right-hand melody, which is to be played gracefully and smoothly.
- Divide the piece into sections for practice. For instance: section 1: measures 1–17; section 2: measures 18–25; section 3: measures 24–38.
- It is very important to release the pedal exactly as indicated.
- The right-hand melody should be slightly brought out above the accompaniment in the left hand.
- Do not take this piece too fast, which will destroy the *tranquillo* mood the composer requests.
- A performance of this piece should be graceful and elegant.

ARAM KHACHATURIAN
(1903–1978, Soviet/Armenian)

Aram Khachaturian was a seminal figure in 20th century Armenian and Soviet culture. Beloved in his homeland for bringing Armenia to prominence within the realm of Western art music, a major concert hall in Armenia's capital Yerevan bears his name, as well as a string quartet and an international competition for piano and composition. Born in Tbilisi, Georgia, of Armenian heritage, he grew up listening to Armenian folk songs but was also exposed to classical music early on through the Tbilisi's chapter of the Russian Music Society, the city's Italian Opera Theater, and visits by musicians such as Sergei Rachmaninoff. He moved to Moscow to study composition in 1921. Khachaturian's musical language combined folk influences with the Russian romantic tradition, embodying the official Soviet arts policy. He used traditional forms, such as theme and variations, sonata form, and Baroque suite forms, in creative ways, juxtaposing them with Armenian melodies and religious songs, folk dance rhythms, and a harmonic language that took inspiration from folk instruments such as the saz. He wrote symphonies, instrumental concertos, sonatas, ballets, and was the first Armenian composer to write film music. Khachaturian's most recognizable composition to the general public is "Sabre Dance" from the ballet *Gayane*. Starting in 1950, he also became active as an internationally touring conductor. He was awarded the Order of Lenin in 1939 and the Hero of Socialist Labor in 1973.

Khachaturian composed two Albums for Children. The first, completed in 1947, included *Adventures of Ivan*. The second volume, composed in 1965, included *Ten Pieces for the Young Pianist*.

Ivan Can't Go Out Today from *Adventures of Ivan*
(composition begun 1926, completed 1947)
Practice and Performance Tips

- The composition expresses the restlessness and melancholy of a sick boy who has to stay in at home.
- Begin practice hands together at a slow, steady tempo.
- Pay careful attention to all of Khachaturian's phrases, accents, and dynamics.
- Learn the notes at a slow tempo before attempting Khachaturian's intricate pedaling.
- Divide the piece into sections for practice. For instance, section 1: measures 1–20; section 2: measures 21–36; section 3: measures 37–50; section 4: measures 51–62; section 5: measures 63–73; section 6: measures 74–86.
- Only increase the tempo in your practice when you have mastered all the details.
- Be sure to keep a steady tempo throughout, until the *ritardando* near the end.

Bedtime Story from *Ten Pieces for the Young Pianist*
(composed 1965)
Practice and Performance Tips

- Practice the right-hand waltz melody separately, finding the smooth *cantabile* (singing tone) the composer indicates.
- Divide the piece into sections for practice. For instance: section 1: measures 1–23; section 2: measures 23–35; section 3: measures 36–55.

- The composer's phrase markings are the key to finding the shape of this graceful, melancholy melody.
- The two chords in the left-hand waltz accompaniment should be played with slight separation.
- The texture of the music changes in the middle section, beginning in measure 23, with the heavy accents in the repeated notes of the right hand.
- The slurred staccatos in the left hand in measures 24, 26 and 28 should be shaped as a phrase, with slight separation.
- The smooth legato tone of the melody returns in measure 36.
- Khachaturian only indicates pedaling in the final measures. By implication, there is to be no pedal used elsewhere.

ROBERT MUCZYNSKI
(1929–2010, American)

Composer and pianist Robert Muczynski studied at DePaul University in his hometown of Chicago with Alexander Tcherepnin. A brilliant pianist, at twenty nine he made his Carnegie Hall debut with a performance of his own compositions. In addition to solo piano works, Muczynski mainly wrote for small chamber ensembles and also composed several orchestral pieces. His flute and saxophone sonatas, as well as *Time Pieces* for clarinet and piano, have become part of the standard repertoire for those instruments. In 1981, his concerto for saxophone was nominated for the Pulitzer Prize. Muczynski was composer in residence on the faculty of the University of Arizona from 1965 until his retirement in 1988.

Diversion No. 1 from *Diversions*, Op. 23
(composed 1967)
Diversions was a follow-up work for student pianists after *Fables*. The level of the set overall is a little more difficult than *Fables* as a whole, though the first piece in *Diversions* is markedly easier than the rest. The composer stated, "I tried not to write down to the student or to the teacher." [1]

[1]From the preface to *Robert Muczynski: Collected Piano Pieces*, G. Schirmer, 1990.

Practice and Performance Tips
- Practice slowly hands separately to begin.
- The composer has put a slur only on the two eighth notes of beat 3 of the first two measures in the right hand, as well as comparable spots (measures 5–6, 18–19, 22–23).
- The above implies that he meant *portato*, or slightly separated, for the eighth notes in those measures not marked with slurs.
- Notice that beat 3 of the left hand is staccato in measures 1–7 and 18–24.
- Muczynski has given very explicit details regarding articulation that should be noted carefully.
- Move to a smooth, legato touch where the notes are marked with a phrase, such as right-hand measures 3–4 and other spots.
- When the opening thematic material recurs at measure 18, it is *p*, and the composer has created interest by writing F-sharp instead of F-natural.
- Except for the specific pedalings indicated, the piece should be played without pedal.
- This music asks for a clean, sensitive touch, and musicality.

Selections from *Fables,* Op. 21 (composed 1965)
This set is subtitled "Nine Pieces for the Young," and was written for an eight-year-old piano student. Each of the fables has a distinct character. Muczynski was an excellent pianist, and his understanding of the instrument is evident in these compositions. About *Fables* the composer stated, "Few people realize how difficult it is to compose a piece that stays within the restrictions of that level. you have to restrain yourself when it comes to key choice, rhythmic complexity, and range. In *Fables* I tried to use strong patterns with the idea of liberating one hand by assigning it a repeating rhythmic or melodic figure." [1]

[1]From the preface to *Robert Muczynski: Collected Piano Pieces*, G. Schirmer, 1990.

Fable No. 1, Op. 21, No. 1
Practice and Performance Tips
- When a composer states non legato as a general direction, that applies to everything except those notes specifically indicated with slurs or phrases.
- Rather than practicing hands separately, in this piece a better practice plan would be hands together at a slow tempo.
- Apply all the details of articulation and dynamics when practicing at a slow tempo.
- Gradually increase the speed over time as you master the music, but always keep a steady beat.
- Notice how the opening material returns, *p* the second time at first, and melodically decorated.
- The composer wrote pedaling only in one spot. By implication he intended the rest of the piece to be played without pedal.
- Be sure to capture the playful fun of this piece.

Fable No. 2, Op. 21, No. 2
Practice and Performance Tips
- Practice hands separately in the beginning, applying the phrasing the composer has written.
- The phrasing, in combination with the dynamics, will give the music shape and grace, and achieve the *espressivo* the composer has indicated.

- Retain the phrasing practiced hands alone when moving to practice with hands together.
- This piece generally asks for a smooth and gentle touch.
- Use no pedal at all.

Fable No. 3, Op. 21, No. 3
Practice and Performance Tips
- Begin practice hands alone, at a slow tempo.
- Learn the articulation from the beginning, along with the notes and rhythms.
- The right-hand melody predominates throughout. It should be slightly brought out over the left hand accompaniment.
- Move to practicing hands together, at a slow practice tempo.
- As you master the notes, rhythms, articulations and dynamics, increase your practice tempo, but always retain a steady beat.
- Notice that the composer has marked *senza pedale* (without pedal), and only indicates pedal on the last chord.

Fable No. 4, Op. 21, No. 4
Practice and Performance Tips
- The graceful melody is in the right hand until measure 22, when it moves to the left hand.
- Bring out the melody slightly over the accompaniment in the other hand.
- Executing the dynamics and phrasing the composer has written will give the melody shape and grace (*grazioso* means graceful).
- In measures 19–21 the left hand must sustain an upper note while playing a lower note staccato on beat 2.
- Use no pedal at all. Muczynski is particular about pedaling in his music. If he had intended the piece to be played with pedal, he would have indicated this.

Fable No. 5, Op. 21, No. 5
Practice and Performance Tips
- Brief as it is, this piece creates a strong dramatic arch, rising from *p* to a climax at *f* then back to *p*.
- Practice the left hand alone, attempting to move from chord to chord very smoothly. Practice without pedal.
- Practice the right hand alone, taking care to shape the melody expressively, using all the articulation, phrasing and dynamics the composer has written.
- When practice begins hands together, do not use the composer's pedaling until you know the piece well.
- The pedaling is quite specific. Notice exactly where the pedal is released and depressed.
- When you know the piece very well, listen to the music in your head and practice the pedal alone.
- Keep this slow adagio steady until the *ritardando* at the end.

OCTAVIO PINTO
(1890–1950, Brazilian)

Octavio Pinto was born in Sao Paulo, Brazil, and enjoyed a successful career as an architect, but he was also an avid music lover, a skillful composer and pianist, and was well-connected to musical life in Brazil. In 1922 he married the famous piano virtuoso Gulomar Novaes, and he was also a close friend of composer Heitor Villa-Lobos. He took lessons for a time from Isidore Philipp, but it was mostly as a composer that his love and talent for music expressed itself throughout his life. He composed piano music, generally character pieces in nature or showpieces, until his death. His most well-known and oft-played work is *Scenas Infantis* (Memories of Childhood) of 1932, which became a signature piece performed by Novaes.

Selections from *Children's Festival: Little Suite for the Piano* (composed 1939)

Little March
The original edition (still available as a Schirmer publication) has optional added octaves in the left hand in measures 17–31, and optional added chords and octaves in the right hand beginning in measure 26 through measure 31. There are also optional added octaves in the right hand for the last two notes of the piece. All these have been eliminated in this edition for the early intermediate level.

Practice and Performance Tips
- The main challenge of this little piece is moving the hands into different ranges of the piano.
- Practice hands separately at a slow tempo before practicing hands together.
- Divide the piece into sections for practice. For instance, section 1: measures 1–16; section 2: measures 17–32; section 3: measures 32–48.
- Except for a few slurred notes, the touch is primarily staccato.
- Play the slurred staccato notes in measures 18 and 22 as slightly separated.
- Pay careful attention to articulation and dynamic changes throughout.
- A march needs an especially steady beat.
- Use no pedal at all.

Serenade
Practice and Performance Tips
- The left hand plays the same pattern throughout.
- Practice the left hand separately, playing smoothly, quietly and evenly.
- The right-hand melody should be more prominent than the left-hand accompaniment.
- Practice the right hand alone, paying attention to the slurs, accents, staccatos, and dynamics, shaping it as a melody.

- The left hand is the foundation and must be very steady throughout.
- Use no pedal at all.

DMITRI SHOSTAKOVICH
(1906–1975, Russian)

A major mid-twentieth century composer, Shostakovich is famous for his epic symphonies, concertos, operas, string quartets, and other chamber works. Born in St. Petersburg, his entire career took place in Soviet-era Russia. His life teetered between receiving high official honors and living with an almost debilitating fear of arrest for works that did not adhere to the Soviet ideals of socialist realism. In 1934, his opera *Lady Macbeth of the Mtsensk District* met with great popular success, but was banned by Stalin for the next thirty years as modernist, surrealist, and obscene. The following year, Stalin began a campaign known as the Purges, executing or exiling to prison camps politicians, intellectuals and artists. Shostakovich managed to avoid such a fate, and despite an atmosphere of anxiety and repression was able to compose an astounding number of works with originality, humor, and emotional power. He succeeded in striking a balance between modernism and tradition that continues to make his music accessible to a broad audience. An excellent pianist, Shostakovich performed concertos by Mozart, Prokofiev, and Tchaikovsky early in his career, but after 1930 limited himself to performing his own works and some chamber music. He taught instrumentation and composition at the Leningrad Conservatory from 1937–1968, with brief breaks due to war and other political disruptions, and at the Moscow Conservatory in the 1940s. Since his death in 1975, Shostakovich has become one of the most performed twentieth century composers.

Selection from *Children's Notebook for Piano*, Op. 69 (composed 1944–45)
Among a huge output of symphonies, operas and chamber music, Shostakovich wrote only a few pieces for piano students. *Children's Notebook for Piano* was written for his eight-year old daughter, Galina, for her studies on the instrument. The original set was published as six pieces. The seventh piece, "Birthday," written for Galina's ninth birthday in 1945, was added in a later edition.

The Mechanical Doll, Op. 69, No. 6
This piece is occasionally known by other translated titles, such as "The Clockwork Doll."

Practice and Performance Tips
- Begin practice hands separately, and at a slow tempo.
- Divide the piece into sections for your practice. For instance: section 1 measures 1–16; section 2 measures 17–29; section 3: measures 30–45.
- Learn the articulation (slurs, staccato, accents) as you learn the notes and rhythms.
- Articulations and phrasings are organically part of the composition, not something added after.
- Move to practicing hands together, at a slow tempo, retaining the articulations you have learned when practicing hands alone.
- Keep a strict tempo, no matter what the speed.
- Be careful to observe the specific dynamics that are composed.
- Use no pedal at all. This music needs a crisp, playful touch throughout. Pedal would spoil the texture.

— Richard Walters, editor
*Joshua Parman, Charmaine Siagian
and Rachel Kelly, assistant editors*

Study for the Left Hand
from *For Children*, Volume 1

Béla Bartók

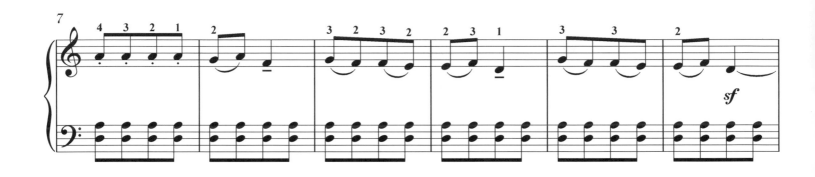

Fingerings are by the composer.

Moon Dance
from *Mountain Idylls*

Alan Hovhaness
Op. 119, No. 2

Fingerings are editorial suggestions.

Forest Nymph
from *For Children*, Volume 2

Béla Bartók

Fingerings are by the composer.

Little March
from *Children's Festival: Little Suite for the Piano*

Octavio Pinto

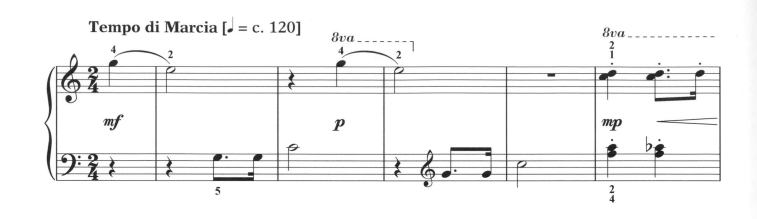

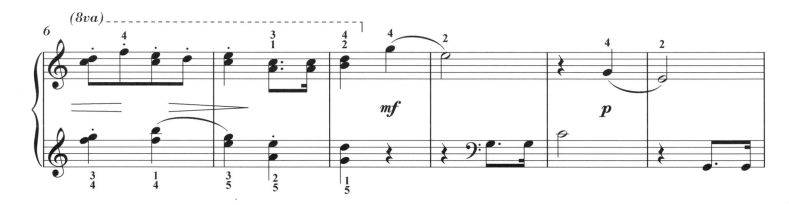

Fingerings are by the composer.
See practice and performance tips for commentary about optional notes eliminated for this edition.

Serenade

from Children's Festival: Little Suite for the Piano

Octavio Pinto

Fingerings are by the composer.

Bedtime Story

from *Ten Pieces for the Young Pianist*

Aram Khachaturian

Fingerings are by the composer.

Birthday Bells
from *At the Piano*, Book 1

Morton Gould

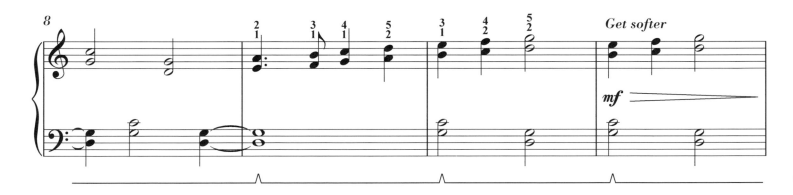

The pedaling is an editorial suggestion.
Fingerings are by the composer.

Almost a Waltz
from *35 Easy Pieces*

Dmitri Kabalevsky
Op. 89, No. 33

Fingerings are by the composer.

A Short Story

from *24 Pieces for Children*

Dmitri Kabalevsky
Op. 39, No. 22

Allegro assai [♩ = c. 120]

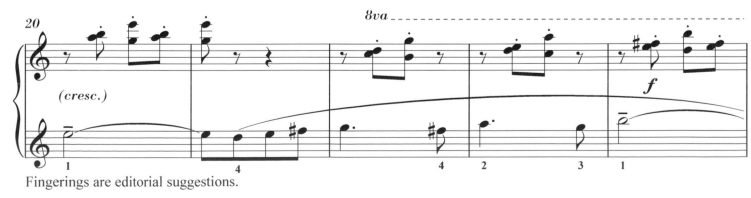

Fingerings are editorial suggestions.

Ivan Can't Go Out Today
from *Adventures of Ivan*

Aram Khachaturian

Fingerings are by the composer.

Toccatina
from *30 Pieces for Children*

Dmitri Kabalevsky
Op. 27, No. 12

Fingerings are editorial suggestions.

Children's Game
from *For Children*, Volume 1

Béla Bartók

Fingerings are by the composer.

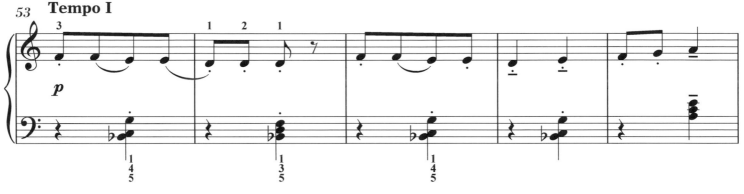

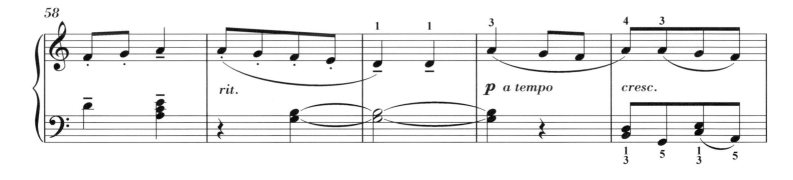

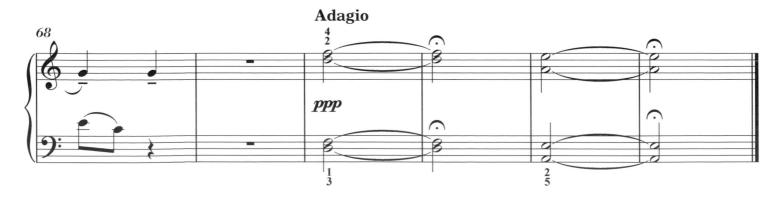

Diversion No. 1
from *Diversions*

Robert Muczynski
Op. 23, No. 1

Fingerings are by the composer.

Slovak Peasant Dance
from *Ten Easy Pieces*

Béla Bartók

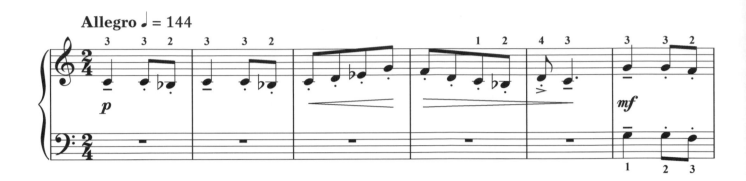

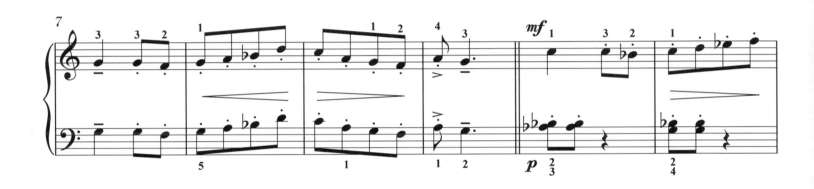

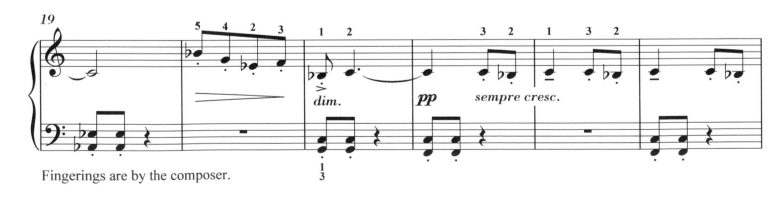

Fingerings are by the composer.

Painful Scuffle
from *Ten Easy Pieces*

Béla Bartók

Fingerings are by the composer.

Rabbit Teasing a Bear-Cub

from *35 Easy Pieces*

Dmitri Kabalevsky
Op. 89, No. 31

Fingerings are by the composer.

To Mark Wansa (age 8)

Fable No. 1
from *Fables*

Robert Muczynski
Op. 21, No. 1

Fingerings are by the composer.

Fable No. 2
from *Fables*

Robert Muczynski
Op. 21, No. 2

Fingerings are by the composer.

Fable No. 3
from *Fables*

Robert Muczynski
Op. 21, No. 3

Fingerings are by the composer.

Fable No. 4

from *Fables*

Robert Muczynski
Op. 21, No. 4

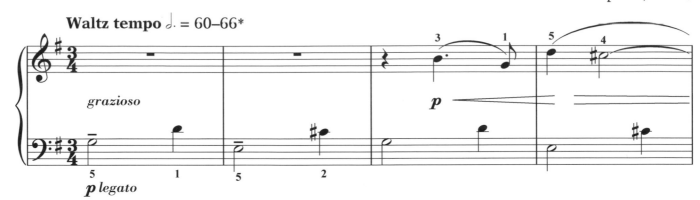

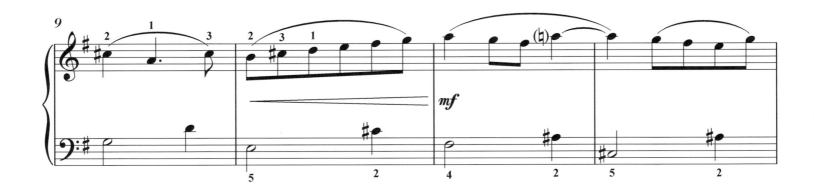

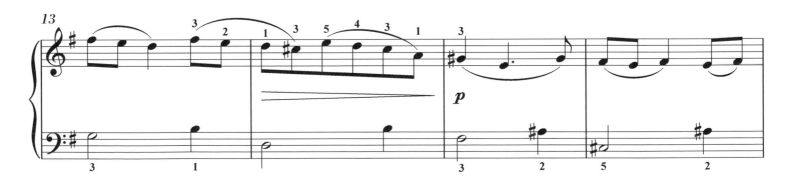

* The composer's original tempo is ♩ = 66, which may be too fast for students; we recommend an alternative.
Fingerings are by the composer.

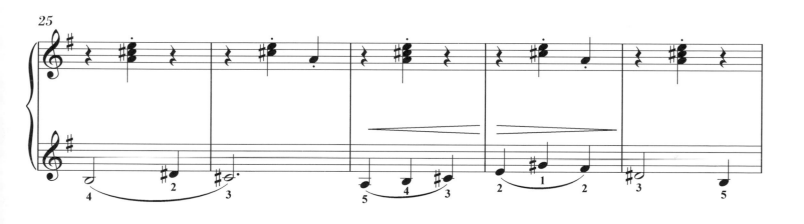

Fable No. 5
from *Fables*

Robert Muczynski
Op. 21, No. 5

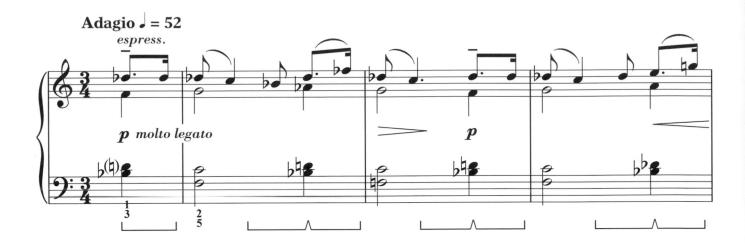

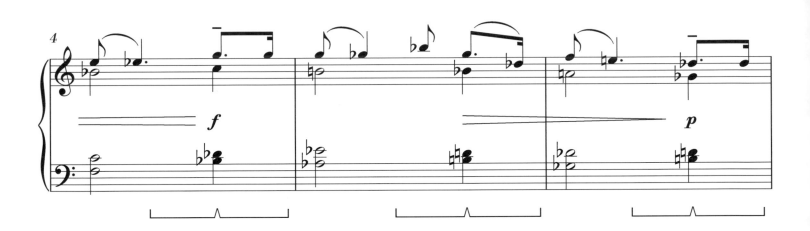

Fingerings are by the composer.

Sad

from *La femme 100 têtes*

George Antheil

Fingerings are editorial suggestions.
* Editor's suggested pedaling.

Toy Dance
from *Five Little Dances*

Paul Creston
Op. 24, No. 3

Fingerings are editorial suggestions.

Children's Dance
from *For Children*, Volume 1

Béla Bartók

Fingerings are by the composer.

Playing Ball
from *30 Pieces for Children*

Dmitri Kabalevsky
Op. 27, No. 5

Fingerings are editorial suggestions.

The Mechanical Doll
from *Children's Notebook for Piano*

Dmitri Shostakovich
Op. 69, No. 6

Fingerings are editorial suggestions.

Sonatina

from *30 Pieces for Children*

Dmitri Kabalevsky
Op. 27, No. 18

Fingerings are editorial suggestions.